CADZOW-HACZOW BOOKS

STEPS TO A MINDFUL LIFE

Martin Stepek was born in Scotland, at Cambuslang near Glasgow on 19 February 1959. He started writing while at school but never sought to publish. Instead he began his career as a company director in his father's family business. It was not until 2012 at the age of 53 that he published his first book, the epic poem *For There is Hope*, followed by *Mindful Living* (2014), *Mindful Poems* ((2015) and *Mindful Living 2* (2015). He collaborated online with the Polish-American poet John Guzlowski, resulting in their joint volume of micro poems *Waiting for Guzlowski* (2017). His latest works are *A Pocket Guide to a Mindful Life* (2018) and *Steps to a Mindful Life* (2018).

By the same author

For There is Hope
Mindful Living
Mindful Poems
Mindful Living 2
Waiting for Guzlowski
A Pocket Guide to a Mindful Life
Steps to a Mindful Life

MARTIN STEPEK
Steps to a Mindful Life

CADZOW-HACZOW BOOKS

CADZOW-HACZOW BOOKS

Published in Cadzow-Haczow Books 2018

Printed in Great Britain
Copyright © Martin Stepek 2018

All rights reserved. No part of this publication may be reproduced, stored in a retrieval system or transmitted in any form or by any means, electronic, mechanical, photocopying or otherwise without permission in writing.

Contents

Introduction....9
Mindfulness is for life not just at class....14
About sublime living.....17
Feeling bad about not worrying....20
Good days, bad days....23
How does your garden grow? 26
How to do more and still feel better....29
Life purpose and meaning....32
No regrets....35
The importance of rest and sleep....38
What is inner peace? 41
Wise mind, tantrum mind....44
Going to the Dentist and other stressful scenarios....47
Different types of attention....50
Altruism - selfishness – self-martyrdom....53
Regaining and maintaining your energy....56
Why am I talking? WAIT – A Mindful practice....59
Real Mindfulness is an antidote to bad business....62
Being in nature as a deep Mindfulness practice....65
Paris: compassion but not shock....68
How would you like your mind to be? 71
Watch where you take your mind....74
Another sort of ambition....77
How much of your day do you live? 80
The impossible but important right now....83
Understand what you can't understand....86

When interruptions take priority....89
Your very own tea ceremony....92
There is no blank slate....95
Lonely at the top - or the perils of making it big....98
Clear understanding, clear practice....101
Getting to really know your emotions....104
When thinking becomes ruminating....107
Mindfulness and Mindfulness training: the difference....110
Understanding yourself.....113
Dealing with negative or difficult people....116
From judging and criticising to reshaping....119
When tired, rest....122
Joy....125
Happiness is a choice, not a result of doing things....128
Who is it that has emotions and moods? 131
Update and restart....134
Work ON your life as well as IN your life....137
The moral philosophy of Mindfulness....140
Freeing yourself wherever you are....143
Conditioning and handling it....146
Deal with issues as if you are drinking tea....149
When something annoying occurs....152

Introduction

Just over a decade ago I had an experience that led to an important change in my life. I've always been a quiet, fairly low-key kind of person. I dislike conflict and I don't like the idea of being well-known. A classic introvert.

So my natural way of living would be to quietly get on with my work and my home life, be relatively passive, accepting life's ups and downs. This didn't mean that I never got anything done. I was successful as a company director, was good at a few sports, and had a fair number of interests. But I wasn't showy or desperate for attention. Quite the opposite.

I had been a member of a Yahoo chat room for a couple of years in the early 2000s. The group's area of interest was the deportation of Polish families to the Soviet Union during the Second World War. Most of the members were the children and grandchildren of survivors; others were the actual survivors, and there were friends of survivors and a few academics.

It was a great group and I learned a lot about what happened to the deportees. This was of importance to me as my father and most of his family were amongst those taken away.

As members of the group got to know each other online, people started to discuss their emotions about the calamity that befell them or their families.
The tone was gentle, intimate and compassionate. It was a pleasure to read what people felt, but I made little contribution. It wasn't my way of doing things.

Then one day one of the group wrote that she had feelings for a grandmother whom she had never met; the grandmother died in a labour camp. The lady asked a very deep and interesting question. What was it she was feeling for someone she never knew? It didn't feel like the love we have for our immediate family. Nor did it feel like the pity we feel for strangers dying of hunger on the TV news. She wrote that she didn't actually know what her feelings were, nor how to describe or express them.

Reading her message I was struck by the fact that I had been writing poems for over twenty years, not to express feelings, for the most part, but just to let out whatever emerged onto the paper. Only after the poem had been born – for that's what it feels like, at least to me, I can't speak for other poets – could I read it and start to understand what it was inside me that had to come out in the form of words.

I felt I could help the lady who wrote the message, or at least tell her that I find out many of my deepest feelings by letting poems and other writings come out without any editing or self-censoring then reading them. So I replied to her message, meaning I was replying to the whole group, a worldwide group of around eight hundred people.

I explained my writing process and said towards the end of my message that many of the poems I had written in the past few years had been about my family's deportation to Russia, or more accurately my reflections and emotions about this.

The cat was out of the bag. "Can you share any of your poems?" I was asked.

I guess I could have said No but, not liking conflict, and not wanting to appear unhelpful and uncaring towards the lady who had started the conversation about her dead grandmother, I decided I had to share a poem.

Looking at the fifty or so poems I had written on this subject by this time, I chose one that I felt best resonated with the story of the lady's grandmother.

It was about my own grandmother. It begins:

Janina I love you
Or rather the thought of you
I cradle your dying body in my arms
Letting you know your family still love you.

I shared it and got a dozen or more responses. How moving it was. How it helped them understand how they felt. How it helped them release long-withheld emotions. How they felt better, healthier, more human for reading it.

The lesson I learned from this brief exchange between strangers over a matter of a few days was this:
Some things I write just might affect another person somewhere in the world in a positive way. Therefore I should share whatever I write. As many poems and reflections as I can get out, in the best way possible so that others might more readily come across them. What matters to me is that maybe even just one individual will feel that it helped them.

So to this book. It is a collection of my weekly newsletter articles which I send out most weeks to regulars who attend my free Hamilton class, and to anyone who signs up for them on my site.

If something in this book contains a spark that ignites a positive difference in a person's life, in a single moment, then the publication of this book will have been worth all the thought and effort it has taken to write and then publish this, and get it out to you.

I have been very fortunate in my life to have received so many messages from people who tell me that some of the things I have written or spoken in my classes and talks have helped them in their lives. So I am confident that this book may bring some of you some degree of insights, comfort, understanding, peace, even joy. I hope that this is the case for you.

Mindfulness is for Life not Just at Class

Mindfulness is variously defined but the most commonly used is "paying attention on purpose in the present moment without judgement".

The vital thing to take from this is that mindfulness is therefore a way of living your life, because the present moment is every moment you have alive, or at least awake. So if you are trying to be mindful during every moment then there's no time that you are happy to ignore the reality of your life in the present moment.

This matters because the way modern scientific mindfulness has developed may lead some people to think it's all about the formal practices people learn in the classic Mindfulness-Based Stress Reduction or Mindfulness-Based Cognitive Therapy (MBSR and MBCT) programmes popularised over the past few decades.

These programmes are great so I intend no criticism, and my views are probably shared by the people who created these programmes. What concerns me is the way the media has portrayed mindfulness, and how that inaccurate view has come to be viewed as the genuine thing.

The misconception is this: that it suffices to do what is called "mindfulness meditation" and you'll feel stress relief or a burden lifted while doing the practice and for some time thereafter.
Then the benefit fades and you need a top up. This is not mindfulness; this is the equivalent of having a massage or sitting in a spa pool.

To use mindfulness like this does work: just as massage or a spa works. But it's like going on a plane to eat the dinner rather than to get you to the destination. It so under-uses its power for good.

To treat or understand mindfulness as a pleasant but temporary "therapy" is to miss out on its full potential to help you become so much happier, healthier, and full of love of life.

That's why I created my weekly class in Hamilton, so that people would not be left trying to become mindful on their own without support after a typical eight week MBSR or MBCT programme; and to repeatedly encourage people to practice being mindful from the moment they wake till their head hits the pillow at night. That's real mindfulness.

Right now you are alive. Notice it. Notice that you are alive; that you feel, touch, hear, see, smell, taste. Notice right now your mental habits as they pop up and disappear. Your prejudices, loves, hates, pettiness, kindness. And from this awareness, this mindfulness, learn to let go of those you see are false or hateful or harmful or unhealthy in any way.

To be mindful is to love life itself, and to appreciate even the challenges we face because being aware of these problems means we are fully alive.

About Sublime Living

I have coined the term "Sublime Living" to try to encapsulate the feeling of joy at just being alive that we can all move towards. I think this is available to us - or at least we can get progressively closer to it - regardless of our current situation, or if we have a religion or philosophy or neither.

One way to try to explain Sublime Living is to show what living is like when it is not sublime. So probably all of us at some time in our lives want something and are not happy because we don't have it. Think of when you wanted a partner but were single, or later wanted freed from your partner, even temporarily, but felt stuck with them.

Or maybe something much more trivial, like wanting a biscuit or a glass of wine but not having any available where you were.

Many times we are frustrated, annoyed or irritated by other people's actions, such as receiving poor service or lack of help from a colleague or family member. Other times we are just caught up in sadness, loneliness, grief, resentment, burning anger or a score of different negative emotions.

Now imagine a life when you could just let go of all these negative feelings because you had the skills to do so and the wisdom to want to.

Imagine further that every so often for no reason other than that it popped up in your mind, you felt a great sense of joy, appreciation and gratitude just for the very fact of being alive.

Imagine you could feel this way even while mourning the loss of a loved one, or while being in physical pain, or if you to someone you loved were suffering a serious illness.

Imagine you felt part of life and were delighted to be part of life.

Imagine you felt you had no need of anything other than the basics of life: food, clothing, a roof over your head, and enough money to pay the basics of life. No craving for a holiday, retail therapy, chocolate therapy, alcohol therapy, any therapy, because when you feel perfectly fine you don't need any therapy.

So we can just sit and be happy, help people as and when we see they need it, enjoy being by ourselves and with others. No need for books or music or TV or films, but happy when they're around too. In other words we don't reject things like the old puritans did but we don't yearn for them all the time like most of us do in today's consumerist culture.

Instead we are just happy. I believe this can be achieved practicing mindfulness in its deepest sense.

Feeling Bad About Not Worrying

My son Iain has had a bad couple of weeks. He is studying for a PhD in Chemistry at a university in Zurich. One of his colleagues had an allergic reaction to a chemical that Iain was using. Then a week later Iain came out in rashes and swelling, all this despite taking all the strict safety instructions.

Iain hasn't yet recovered, nor is he free from concern about how the two contaminations arose.

In one respect this is a classic worrying time not just for him, but for my wife, daughter and I as family.

We all know that worrying does no good. We also know, though we don't explore this as much, that it actually does us harm. It eats up our time, it tires us mentally and physically, and it puts a grey, dark cloud over everything in our lives. Not exactly the best self-created mood we can achieve as people.

But there is one other aspect about these kind of situations that further get in the way of us having an enjoyable life. Guilt. Feeling good about life even though something not good is happening.

I'm pretty sure we all do this. Some people do it to extremes. Even someone as wise as the Buddha is alleged to have said "How can there be laughter when the world is burning?" (he meant burning with violence, suffering etc

I used to come across this when I was involved in politics. Well-meaning, but somewhat over-zealous, righteous people ready to put a stop to any enjoyment because of the usual terrible news on TV each day. So it is with my family just now. How dare we have a good time while our son is in pain and concerned about his work?

But we did. My wife, daughter and I had booked a table at Chatelherault Country Park on Sunday evening, to see an open air performance of Hamlet. It was superb; not just dramatic and thought-provoking, but lots of funny bits too. The sun even shone (thought it got cold by the time it finished, and the midges were adding to the tragedy!)

So we managed the unacceptable; to feel good even though there's bad news around us.

It wasn't a temporary escape, or at least not for me. It's mental training. A recognition that life is best served by you being happy and enthusiastic. So you do what you can to resolve a problem, but at the same time you mindfully notice if negativity seeps into your mind and threatens to take you over.

Learn the skill of letting mental poison slip away. Life is far too precious to waste moments which could be full of appreciation, fun and enjoyment. Moreover the people around you are too precious for you to ruin their moments by your uncontrolled negative mind. Mindfulness is not just about you.

Good Days, Bad Days

There's no such thing as a good day. Or a bad day. Every day is made up of thousands of moments. You might think of a moment as about a second long, or if it reflects something happening over a short period of time, maybe you'd stretch your meaning of a moment to say twenty seconds.

If a moment lasts a second then we have about 58,000 moments in our waking day. Even if each moment lasts twenty seconds we still have almost three thousand moments in a day.

Not many of us will ever have experienced a day where every single moment was good, or bad. Yet we might have considered a day to be either one or the other. When we do that what is actually happening is that our mind compiles the most notable moments of the day and tricks us into thinking that the feeling of those best or worst moments somehow transformed all the other moments in our day.

This isn't just a curious thing. It's part of the serious problem of how we view ourselves, other people, our lives, our work, our colleagues, everything.

Instead of seeing the reality - a moment, an incident, a few words spoken - we exaggerate it a thousand-fold so that a few bad moments becomes a whole bad day. Or someone's behaviour once or twice for a few minutes makes them useless, untrustworthy, an enemy or whatever.

In short our mind, for the sake of simplifying everything to make it more understandable, condemns us to inaccurate, biased perceptions, with most things we think being way out of proportion to reality. This affects how we feel about our day, ourself, those around us, the weather, everything.

We make poor decisions because we don't see clearly. We have low opinions of others because we can't see past their few failings or errors of judgement. We think someone's work is mistaken because our own view of it is skewed. Worst of all we think a whole day is bad when in fact a few moments didn't go our way, and this down mood affects us negatively for the rest of the day, maybe even spilling into the next few days.

Meanwhile our life keeps passing us by moment by moment.

We not only miss these moments by being so consumed by faulty thoughts and feelings, we actually poison the moments, making them worse for those we are with as well as for ourselves. In doing so we train our mind to think that way in future, so a vicious circle is developed.

There is only one way of this trap; training your mind to be fully engaged with life, moment by moment. It is easy to say, much harder to do. But if we are to live as fully, successfully, and constructively as we have the potential to do, then we must aim to be mindful, to be fully with the moment, and the next and the next.

How Does your Garden Grow?

We're having a new front garden created right now. We talked about the need for a new drive first of all, a few years ago. We then added our wish to have a new lawn because the front grass was full of moss and we just couldn't solve that issue. Finally a year or so ago we made what was for us a very big decision - to have the whole front garden redesigned and laid out afresh.

So we talked with a professional garden designer several months ago and after really interesting discussions agreed a design plan which she drew.

The designer then recommended landscapers to do the job and this too was agreed. This was all before Christmas.

As often happens various things -weather, other job priorities, holidays - got in the way and delayed the start of the work until last Monday 8th June.

First thing was to protect or keep aside all we wanted to keep from the original garden. Then everything else had to be dug up, dug out, lifted or scraped away and put in a skip (though both neighbours got some slabs).

The first couple of days the place looked like a site... because that's what it was. But now a week later we have a beautiful outline, new driveway, couple of boulders, a nice special feature, and top soil ready for the week ahead.

This week is replanting what we wanted to keep, and after that choosing then planting new plants.

And that's just the beginning. We have the new framework, some of the key things we want in position but it'll be years before the plan comes to fruition, as the new plants slowly mature. And the garden will take its own shape, despite our plans.

This is what mindfulness practice is to the mind. We need to recognise firstly that our mind isn't all we'd like it to be. We need to want a new, better mind, one designed with more thought and consideration; and we also need some guidance on how to get the mind we want. But we'll do the work it entails.

After this, keeping on wanting the new mind doesn't help. What works is getting the job done, and yes at the beginning it can seem like a total mess, like a building site, not a garden. Accept this.

Even when we have done some of the heavy work, with stones, cobbles, soil, all we've really done is laid out the sections. So with mindfulness. We get to understand things a bit better, feel the benefits and calmness. But it takes years of planting and nurturing, watering and weeding to slowly reshape the mind so it flowers and develops to be the mind we truly want. So be patient and don't yearn for the end result. It'll come if you do the mindful work.

And of course there will always be weeding to do!

How to do More and Still Feel Better

For those in the workplace there is a seemingly never-ending pressure to do more, often with less support or help. And it's much the same at home. Somehow we have accumulated more and more things to do, and it seems to have no end.

So what can we do about this?

There are a few things. Firstly develop the classic mindfulness view: you can only live in the present moment. So you can only ever be doing one thing at a time. See what your most important or urgent task is and just do it. Try not to think of all the other stuff until you've done the first job.

Secondly be self-aware, especially of how you feel. Tiredness and stress can sneak up on us, and we often find ourselves working through them for hours. But this simply reduces our productivity. We think we're working hard but in fact we're working at a poor level and at a poorer pace. We just don't recognize it. This is a classic macho male attitude though women often fall prey to it too.

Thirdly, take frequent breaks, go for a walk, even if it's literally for two minutes, preferably outside.

The fresh air blows tiredness away. You lose time to work when you take a break but this is more than compensated by the energy you regain.

The statistics on fatigue and burn out at work are horrific worldwide. People slowly wear themselves out, so slowly that they don't see their own decline, and continue to think they're fine. It's only when their energy levels get so low that something gives, usually physical first, but increasingly mental.

The irony is that this is often the results of a culture of well-meaning so-called "hard work", a kind of downward spiraling treadmill, which once you've started on it, you find it hard to come off.

In the legal profession, where I now work this is a particular problem, much to the surprise of many people. In America a lawyer is 3.6 times more likely to suffer from depression than other workers. It's similar in Australia and NZ. Here in Scotland of all the calls to a lawyer helpline in 2014 84% were about stress.

When I discuss mindfulness with people in workplaces there are always two polarized responses: one group get it immediately and say how helpful it is practically for them.

Another group are cynical, skeptical – even when you explain about Harvard and Oxford and the world leading neuroscientists' work on mindfulness – and think practices like mindfulness have no place in the workforce.

These are the people I am most concerned about. The ones who are open-minded seek and get help. Those who can't see there's a problem are usually the ones who have or in fact *are* the problem.

Life Purpose and Meaning

If you are religious this particular article might in many ways be irrelevant to you. After all, most religions have very clear statements of what the purpose of life is, and what a meaningful life consists of. Your task is to follow those teachings.

But in another sense of course many people who have faith in a religion might know the stated purpose or meaning of life but still struggle to turn that understanding into everyday practice. I guess if that wasn't the case we'd have billions of perfect and perfectly happy people around the world, and that clearly doesn't seem quite true does it?

Then there's the rest of us. The doubters, the uncertain, the agnostics, the atheists, and the just plain "never really thought about it" group. For many in these groups the challenge is to find a meaning, a purpose of our own making. And that's a bit messy, given that we're all a combination of different wants and drives and conscience and greed and love and pettiness. Hard to collate all those mental creations into a coherent philosophy (if that's what we mean by the purpose of life).

For me the answer lies in getting away from ideas and concepts *about* life, and instead focusing on *actual* life. Actual life is not an idea; it is served up to us on a plate, like a gift, in each moment we're awake. We don't need a purpose to be alive. Nor do we need some grand philosophy to experience raw life in all its vigour in that moment.

What we call a life is a mental creation too. None of us live something called "my life". What we mean by "my life" is an idea, a mental picture signifying a period of time from the moment we were born to the moment we die. See how unreal that is, except as a story or a narrative. You don't actually live a life at all. You live one moment. It passes. Then you live the next moment. And so on until you don't live another moment. That's what we call being dead.

In fact therefore you don't actually *die*. One moment you are alive. The next moment you are already dead. There isn't some bit in between called dying, except again as something we've created as an idea in our mind.

Which leaves what we can experience. Being alive in the pure uncluttered moment. And that to me is the purpose we all have.

To experience the moment fully. To give to it all you can, and to take from it all it has to offer. This is as applicable to religious people as to the non-religious.

I add in two simple ethical guidelines. Help other living things if I can. Try to do no harm to any living thing if I can avoid it. Each person has to work out their own code of conduct. And if I screw up, try again in the next moment.

For me that's it. All we ever have is a moment. My purpose is to experience it and respond to it as best I can. And that's meaningful enough for me.

No Regrets

We've all done things in the past which, looking back, we regret having done. Or we look back and regret that something was done to us.

Regret is the mental state of wishing that something never happened. Not a particular practical state of mind because we can't undo the past. We are stuck with our past, our decisions, our choices, and we are stuck with whatever has happened to us or been done to us.

We can choose to live with the past though that is in many ways a contradiction in terms. The past is gone. We live in the present so we can't actually live *with* the past. We can only dwell on past events from time to time.

The way of being we call Mindfulness considers regret as unhealthy use of our time. The fluid ever-changing present, that remarkable thing we call "Now" is a gift to us if we choose to see it that way.

My first teacher of mindfulness, an elderly Canadian psychologist who had become a Buddhist monk in one of the Tibetan traditions, once said to me the following statement:

"Reality is a field of potential"

Reality only exists in the present moment, not in our thoughts or fears for the future, nor in the multitude of memories we call the past.

So if reality only exists in the present we can take my teacher's words and say

Each moment is a field of potential

In other words each moment presents us with an opportunity to use in any way that is possible.

Think of how you can use the next few moments that come racing up to us after you read this. You could just be aware that you are alive, able to notice your own existence. You could stop and enjoy the physical sensation of breathing in, breathing out, the cool freshness of air going into your body, the slow rise and fall of your rib cage as the lungs fill and empty.

Or you could focus on your current situation and see what might be possible. Can you get a drink of water, tea, coffee, and savour it? Can you see something beautiful? What can you hear? What can you do to make right now to make your life good, or reduce its suffering if you have any? Or what, right now, could you do to help someone around you? A random act of kindness perhaps.

Regrets? With the gift of this moment, this field of potential, who would choose to despoil it with regret for something we can't change, when we could create something of joy, beauty, goodness.

The Importance of Rest and Sleep

Apart from breathing it's the thing we do most in our life - sleep. The average person sleeps between seven and nine hours sleep each day, meaning that it we live to seventy-five years old we will have slept for twenty-five years.

Most of the things that happen in our body and mind have evolved to do so for important reasons, namely survival or reproduction. To sleep for a third of the time we're alive suggests that it is of absolutely crucial importance to our survival and wellbeing.

Yet we think nothing of it.

Mindfulness of course is all about noticing, paying attention to what's actually going on inside and around us, from moment to moment. When we start to do this as a newly developed practice one of the many things we notice is how tired we actually are.

Sometimes it takes us a while - weeks or months, even years - before we notice this because we are so used to being tired we no longer recognise what not being tired feels like.

But slowly we start to notice things; our eyes in particular can be a bit strained, tired, not fresh and alive and alert. Our face feels drab, unanimated, slow to respond to thing, and doesn't light up readily.

Our body follows suit. Slow, almost reluctant to get going in the morning or at work or home.

Then we start to notice our habits. We work through tiredness instead of taking a short walk outside for some much-needed fresh air. We skip doing a two minute - just two minute - mindfulness breathing exercise because it's too much bother. We drink precisely the wrong things just before bed - coffee, alcohol - while we're watching a stimulating film or TV programme. These are things that make it less likely that we'll sleep well.

So do these three things today and all this week:
Notice how your mind feels right now.
Notice how parts of your body feel right now.
Notice what you eat, drink, watch on TV tonight.

We almost all know how to live well so I won't repeat the obvious. To notice - to be mindful - is the vital first step. Then we have true choice on how to respond to whatever we find when we notice.
We have escaped from automatic living and are now liberated for at least that one moment.

When we sleep well, when we are fully rested and refreshed we are a different person. Happier, healthier, more thoughtful and considerate, and approach life more lightly and with greater good humour. Why settled for the opposite and why impose that opposite on those around you.

What is Inner Peace?

It's a term that is widely banded about. Inner Peace. For many of us when we've had a bad day the idea of inner peace may come across as like a place of refuge, escape, to get away from all the stress and anger or frustration we feel pulsing rapidly inside us.

Or on more reflective days the words Inner Peace may cause us to think of places like India, with images of yogis sitting cross-legged with their eyes closed. Think Beatles 1967.

For me Inner Peace is neither of these things. It's a kind of pillar-like core, almost physical in feeling, felt mostly in my abdomen and upper stomach area, and sitting too in the part of my body where the lungs and heart are.

This is a bit strange as we usually think of who we are and what we feel as being located in our head, where the brain is.

Inner Peace doesn't go away when you are frazzled by life's inevitable challenges and upsets. You still feel its strength and solidity in your body. It isn't therefore a place you go to for time out because it's already there, all the time. You just need to become aware of it and it settles things down. That's being mindful of course.

And Inner Peace is nothing to do with being mystical or "alternative" or spirituality in usual senses of these words.

Inner Peace is remaining happy when you're not, in love with life when you think that life is crap, accepting all the ups and downs when you are trying to run away from all these things.

Inner Peace just is. It doesn't go away once we've achieved it, though we can forget it's there when we're too wrapped up in our own miseries or false views about life.

Mindfulness builds inner peace. It develops qualities of mind in our brains so that we assess the junk that our mind produces – about 90% of the total in my case, maybe more – and lets that lot fade away without being trapped by it while it lasts.

If we want Inner Peace it will take longer to develop. The mind is quick to spot yet another longing or yearning and make a mental habit of it. We should consciously and deliberately try to minimize our wants, to reduce "wanting" as a habit in our lives. Inner Peace is the opposite of wanting.

When we want we're not at peace. When we have Inner Peace we don't want anything.

Wise Mind, Tantrum Mind

The original title I had chosen for this piece was Big Mind and Little Mind, straight from Zen. But the insight that we have competing views within our mind of any situation is not the preserve of a particular philosophy. Those of us who had the privilege of growing up watching Tom and Jerry cartoons will remember the twin images that popped up in Jerry's mind from time to time, a wee devil mouse on the left, and a corresponding angel mouse on the right, of course giving him totally opposing advice on what to do in a particular moment.

I've called them Wise Mind and Tantrum Mind because that's how I've come to know them in my own years of practicing mindfulness and trying to live it moment by moment.

My Tantrum Mind sneaks in and grows ever-bigger whenever I am ruminating on something that is in any way annoying, whether it's trivial, like forgetting to being something to work from home, or something major like bad news concerning a family member or close friend.

The Tantrum Mind has a very clear philosophy: everything should conform to my wishes and be aligned with whatever I happen to be doing at any moment every single day I am alive. When it doesn't – me forgetting something, a family member dying – I take a tantrum of sorts.

That's what a tantrum is; getting upset because the world has not conformed to your wishes at that moment.

Pathetic, isn't it? But that's how I am.

Thank goodness I have a Wise Mind too, even if it isn't so ready to rush to advise me as my ever-prepared Tantrum Mind. When, with mindfulness, and the other stuff we know is good for our mind – good nutrition, water, fresh air, exercise, nature – we strengthen our Wise Mind, it becomes better at coming to our rescue from the amazingly volatile and petty Tantrum Mind. At its best, it lets all that woeful stuff go even before it has had the chance to take you over for its mercifully short lifespan.

This leaves you with a wonderful clear, peaceful and refreshed mind, ready to think through what's best in any given moment, any particular situation.

The Tantrum Mind can be reduced in energy, thwarted even at its peak, controlled, managed, even partially tamed. In some instances it can even be wiped out, and what a great feeling it is to be aware that a certain recurring awful series of thoughts no long appear in your mind.

This is what aiming for mindfulness moment to moment, day to day can do for you. It is really quite remarkable, so keep up your own efforts and try to enjoy it, moment by moment, thought by thought.

Going to the Dentist and Other Stressful Scenarios

I'm actually OK with going to the dentist. I look on it as a way of keeping well or resolving problems. I don't get stressed at the thought of going.

Which is just as well as a couple of weeks ago a major crown and filling came out. Then, a week after it was sorted, another filling came out.

I'm going to the dentist today.

Last time the treatment took about fifteen to twenty minutes. Not as long as some major work but longer than the usual check-up or small filling.

I moved in and out of mindfulness whilst I was being treated last time. At times when I'm actually being treated I do feel the anxiety, the fear, the anticipation of pain.

So from moment to moment I tried to place my attention on my breathing. This is a classic mindfulness practice. Instead of allowing my mind to focus on the tooth which the dentist was working on I tried to notice the quality of my breath.

Once I had established the new locus of attention I tried to deliberately enjoy or appreciate the sensations that come with the breath. The sense of life and energy that an in-breath brings. The calming, slow down feeling on an out-breath.

Then I tried to deliberately slow down each breath so that it enhanced the appreciation of the sensations associated with breathing.

All of these practices are to be done very quietly. Gently. Subtly. This is the effortless effort we describe in mindfulness.

When the breath is consciously recalibrated in this way the mind seems to notice the body more readily.

My body automatically tightens when I'm having treatment at the dentist. Once I notice it I see its finer details.

My chest tightens, almost locks. My shoulders stiffen as if expecting a blow. My stomach muscles are clenched.

Adrenalin is pumping. I feel it course through my body.

As I notice each unpleasant physical sensation I deliberately try to allow my body to loosen up. I lower the shoulders. I release the chest. And the stomach muscles.

I have found that if you watch your adrenalin in a relaxed way it will slow down of its own accord.

Try these techniques during any time you feel stressed. If you have time try them now.

Different Types of Attention

Mindfulness is paying attention on purpose to what's actually going on in the present moment, without the usual inner views, opinions or judgements.

It is one of many types of attention. Our lives can be transformed if we learn what different types of attention we experience, how to nurture the finest types and how to let go of the worst.

The default type of attention experienced by people is obedience to whatever the mind creates. We can label this Slave Attention. The mind responds to a situation with anger and we become angry. Our attention is angry attention.

We didn't choose this type of attention. The mind created the emotion and we just followed it without question. We are literally slaves to our mind. The mind is a volatile and irrational master.

There are some important sub-types of Slave Attention. One of the worst, especially for those in work or who are carers, is Exhausting Attention.

This occurs when we have to focus close attention on something. For some people, especially those with desk jobs and painstaking work, this can become your habitual state of mind at work. It is an attempt to force the mind to drill down deeper and deeper. The neck tightens. The shoulders rise and become cramped. Most of all the brow furrows and the eyes tense up.

This excessive mental and physical effort drains both mind and body. It leads to a semi-permanent stress, exhaustion and unhappiness.

Another sub-type of Slave Attention is Daydreaming, or fantasising. This can be very pleasant. It often features imagined scenes of triumph, success, hot holidays, revenge, and of course sex.

In this form of Slave Attention we go willingly but unthinkingly to where the mind leads, enjoying it as if it is our own private novel or soap opera.

There are a few problems with this and other types of attention. Firstly they are not chosen by you but selected by your mind. You have not had a say in whether or not to go along with the direction of the mind. That's why I call it Slave Attention.

In contrast Mindful Attention is very light. It has none of the qualities of Exhausting Attention.

It chooses after quiet reflection on what the mind produces automatically. Sometimes it can consciously go along with what the mind creates, but only after due consideration. So it is very clear.

It is also very considerate of others. It lets go of destructive or unhealthy creations of the mind. Finally it is calm and rested. It has no trace of effort yet it is highly productive, rational and creative.

Altruism - Selfishness – Self-martyrdom

We are all born with a similar array of possible responses to different situations. These include anger, frustration, good humour, laughter, kindness, tolerance, hatred, and love.

How these potential responses become character traits or habits in each of us is down to our unique combination of genes and then life experiences.

Amongst these many aspects of human behavior are altruism, selfishness and what I call self-martyrdom. I'd like to explore and compare these.

Altruism is a state of mind which wants to help someone or something without looking for anything in return. It can become acts of kindness, generosity, love. Most people would think of such a state of mind as one of our highest human qualities. In politics one thinks of Gandhi, Martin Luther King, or Nelson Mandela.

Selfishness is probably the most powerful default driver in our mind. All those times we get annoyed it's because something didn't happen the way we wanted it to. Same with frustration or minor irritation. And when we feel impatient it's because something isn't happening at the speed or time we want it to.

This spark of almost toddler-like reactions to little things in life happen several times a day. They are so quick and so frequent we don't even register them for what they are.

Self-martyrdom is often mistaken for altruism or love, and people are often praised for such activity. But it is a false positive trait, and leads to unhappy and often destructive results.

It is most often seen in two areas: care for family members, and over-commitment to an employer.

People wear themselves out looking after parents, children or spouses. As a result they usually die a few years earlier than they otherwise would have.

Moreover the quality of time they have with the person they are martyring themselves for is usually poor, because the carer is so tired and dissatisfied.

So it is poor use of time, with unhealthy results.

It is a similar situation at work. Some people sacrifice themselves on the altar of success or loyalty. This leads to tiredness, poor thinking, and poor communication. So although the hours are devoted to work, the quality is harmed.

There is a sane path to be taken. A path that optimizes personal health and happiness, family care, and appropriate commitment to work.

To see this path we need our mind to be clear and calm, compassionate towards others but also self-compassionate. Mindfulness develops such a mind.

Regaining and Maintaining your Energy

I can't speak for everyone but for me being tired is the most debilitating common mental state I experience.

Very few of us nowadays get physically tired. Unless you are training hard for an event or play a sport to a high level, physical exhaustion is rare.

It's mental tiredness that is the challenge.

So how do we handle this?

Firstly there are preventatives: getting sufficient sleep; avoiding food, drink and entertainment in the evening that over-stimulate or affect quality of sleep; avoiding sweet or overly-fatty foods and drinks during the daytime; getting out into the fresh air especially in natural surroundings.

Then there are the sustainers of energy, and note that most of these are directly mindful or related to mindfulness: doing one thing at a time; doing it slowly; doing it with a clear, light mind; stopping to notice your breathing every so often; having a glass of water or a cup of green tea, and taking the time to drink it attentively and appreciatively; getting up and going for a walk if you feel your energy dipping just a little.

Finally there are the rechargers of energy. These are similar to the other categories above. Note that there are quick rechargers and slower more sustaining rechargers.

Quick rechargers include focussing on the breath for up to a minute or two; getting out in the fresh air, especially if it's windy or raining; holding a smile for around ten or twenty seconds.

Longer-lasting rechargers include deep, longer mindfulness sitting; having a nap; going for a long walk or run or swim or bike ride; and eating a healthy meal.

Apart from the obvious issue of feeling tired and lethargic, the biggest problem with feeling lacklustre is the effect it makes our your mood.

When we are tired we tend to be grumpier, shorter-tempered, irritable. We dislike interruptions more than normal, and we listen much more poorly than when we feel fine.

So allowing our energy levels to drop has an impact on the quality and speed of what we do and also on how we feel about the world around us, while causing our relationships with people to decline.

So weigh up the list of things I have noted as preventatives, sustainers and rechargers of energy, and by inference, what drains your energy. See how much of what we habitually do are things that reduce our energy and spirits. Notice how difficult or easy it would be to put some of these into action in your everyday life. Do try some of these today - notice the difference.

Why am I Talking? WAIT – A Mindful Practice

I was in a meeting this morning with a very interesting woman who is a life coach. We were talking about family businesses, and the general tendency of people in families to just talk over one another. We also discussed the fact that some individuals just dominate conversations, while others can't get in a word in.

I noticed my own habit of wanting to speak and interrupt the other person just as they are coming to the end of a sentence – without stopping to consider whether the other person had another sentence or two to share.

This is something we're all guilty of, some of us more than others.

It is hard to listen properly for a sustained period. Our mind just churns out ideas, thoughts, responses while others are talking.

I first learned about listening as a skill we can learn from a Harvard University professor who came to do a workshop on family business around 1995 at Glasgow Caledonian University.

He said something that has stuck with me ever since.

"Most people don't listen. They just reload."

Listening is not only the way to understand what someone is saying. It is also a matter of paying proper respect to the other person.

I read somewhere yesterday about the practice which makes up the title of this article. I can't remember who wrote the piece or who originated the acronym. It's a good one:

WAIT

Why Am I Talking?

It is a perfect mindfulness practice to ask yourself that question, as you are about to speak or while you're talking.

We talk without thinking.
We talk without thinking whether our contribution would add anything of worth.
We talk instead of listening.
We talk instead of allowing silence to enter into the conversation; the silence that allows deeper or more intimate emotions to emerge as words.

The desire to be heard needs to be balanced with the potential to be present with another in silence.

And when we practise mindfulness we practise listening to ourselves, to what our mind is saying.

Real Mindfulness is an Antidote to Bad Business

In the sometimes insular world of mindfulness professionals there's a big debate going on about whether mindfulness is helping business and other organisations become more ethical and better places to work at; or if in fact the opposite is happening - that mindfulness is being diluted and bent out of its original moral shape to serve big business's drive for ever-greater growth and profits.

Authentic mindfulness starts from the view of the wellbeing of all. More than that it sees all life as *equally* deserving of wellbeing, and deserving of *equal* levels of wellbeing.

Thus mindfulness is inherently against harm or destruction of people, place, planet. It exists to help tame our natural greed and self-centredness, replacing these with a clear, calm, *universally* compassionate mindset. In this regard it is the complete opposite mindset and culture of the stereotype we associate with big business.

The current scandals engulfing Volkswagen and FIFA would be inconceivable in a corporate culture that is deeply mindful.

The idea in the case of Volkswagen that one would create software to communicate a global mass lie about carbon emissions - something that is life-threatening for almost all species, is astonishing even in the often grubby world of big business.

The succession of scandals and massive personal payouts at FIFA, the supreme organisation of football, the world's most popular sport, is so degrading of the image of something billions of people love, it is hard to believe people did this.

In contrast mindfulness nurtures the exact opposite of these actions. In clearly seeing any situation mindfulness impels us to ask these questions:

"Am I sure I should be doing this?"

"What will be the impact on others of doing this?"

"Does this potentially harm anyone or anything?"

It imposes a challenging culture on all organisations, a culture that should be in all their vision and values statements, in their inductions and training and development of all of their people:

A culture of no harm
A culture of nurturing all life, including the planet

A culture of being part of society, not exploiting it
A culture of driving positive change in their industry
A culture of reducing salary differentials
A culture of full and transparent tax payments

This is what a truly mindful organisation looks like. If it doesn't look and feel like this it is not mindful, or it is not yet developed enough in its culture change to be described as an organisation with a mindfulness culture. Sadly we have few organisations of this stature.

Being in Nature as a Deep Mindfulness Practice

We all know that walking is good for us.

Being in nature is available for most of us too. Walking in nature gives an added element but most of the benefits of being in nature come to us whether we can walk or not. Just being in nature is itself healing and nurturing.

Unless we are not really in nature whilst we are there.

How often are we not really present?

How often do we miss the raw experience of life, of being alive right here in this place where we happen to be? Are you fully present right now?

In this moment with all that is present in it?

I walked round Strathclyde Loch this morning with my wife. It was a long walk, over an hour. That gave us time to be mindful of each other, mindful with each other.

It still left us plenty of time to be mindful of all that nature in that area gave to us.

With our eyes we saw the majesty of autumn colours. The elegance of swans. The beauty of bullrushes against the backdrop of the glassy loch.

The impressive darkness of three cormorants with their wings spread wide as they stood on rocks sticking out above the water.

We heard the sounds of walkers' steps, cyclists' bikes, couples talking. Bird songs. An ebb and flow of sound that followed us subtly as we walked round the loch. Soothing sounds in the air.

We felt at the start of the walk the slight chill of the October morning on our cheeks and hands. Its sharpness. Its power.

As we walked our bodies warmed up. So did the air. We felt the gentler warmer flow of air on our skin.

We felt our steps. Measured, not slow, not rushed, on the path. Our trainers kept the steps soft.

It is easy to lapse when walking. To fall into ruminating about concerns, life plans, thoughts of work. Our mind naturally leans that way.

It is so easy to lose the miracle of being in nature. Of being part of nature. Of being nature itself.

But when we are fully there, with it, being it, we can be completely at peace. In love with life itself. Aware and appreciative of the gift of being alive.

It is so easy to lock ourselves indoors. It's too cold, too wet, too dark outside. We're busy, too tired.

When we let these thoughts rule us we lose life. We lose everything. Try to practice mindfulness, to lead the mind to being out in nature as much as you can.

Paris: Compassion but Not Shock

We are easily shocked.

If the news is violent and comparatively nearby, the shock increases.

The terrible news from Paris was both violent and geographically close to us. France is one of the most popular places in the world for Scots and other British citizens to visit. Paris is a much-loved venue for a city-break. Disneyland Paris is a draw for so many families from our country. So it's all very familiar territory.

The philosophy behind mindfulness offers two seemingly contrasting responses to such news: deep compassion for those who have suffered; and a dispassionate examination of our natural instinctive reactions to the event.

Compassion is one of our highest human qualities. The combination of empathy - an understanding of how the other feels - and sympathy - the offer of support and solidarity, is deeply moving to experience personally and to witness in others.

Non-judgmental observation of our mental state is entirely different. It recognises that shock and upset at the awful events are not healthy for us, however natural these feelings are.

Major news incidents like this one can draw us away from the reality of the present moment, sometimes for days on end. Thus our gut response can destroy our whole focus on life for that time.

Moreover, it almost always leads us to wrong and deeply unhealthy conclusions. I've witnessed it on social media several times in the past 24 hours. A common response is that the world is getting worse, more dangerous, more unpredictable. That travel is now risky.

The sad reality is that incidents like this, and other more natural disasters are an everyday occurrence. The existence of dramatic footage and its proximity to our country give it that magnified feeling. But almost every day in Syria, Iraq, Afghanistan similar numbers are being killed. Literally thousands of children are dying needlessly of disease and hunger every day.

So, shocking though it appears to us, sadly this is how the world is; and tragically for Paris, it was its misfortune to be the most recent case of human violence to its own kind. Accept this as a sad reality.

Another response is to leap to unprovable and often factually incorrect conclusions, political or social, about causes or responses to such events.

The practice of mindfulness helps us be more compassionate and less judgmental and shockable, all at the same time. This allows us to be humane, open to others while getting such events in truer perspective, and we remain content and at peace.

How Would you Like your Mind to be?

To want something implies that you lack it just now.

To want happiness or peace of mind may be the single biggest obstacle to attaining it.

Both of these are not helpful states of mind.

One paradox about learning how to harness our mind: to want a particular mental result often requires pretending that we don't want it at all.

Another paradox: to be content does not mean ridding the mind of unhealthy thoughts or feelings.

The two core elements of mindfulness are noticing and accepting. Let's examine these in turn.

In mindfulness we train ourselves to notice what's actually going on, especially in our own minds.

Actually, this is not literally possible. According to one psychologist we have around 50,000 mental ideas, thoughts, feelings, reactions every day.

Our thoughts therefore arise so fast and so frequently we can't notice them all, let alone learn to handle them.

But that's OK as we're not seeking to achieve anything. We're just training and practising.

As we train ourselves to be more mindful we learn to notice more of our mind's responses and thoughts. It doesn't matter how many more.

Simultaneously we learn to better accept what our mind creates rather than hating it, denying it, defending it, or running away from it.

As a result over time we become increasingly familiar with the way the mind works and what it produces. We see its recurring habits and reactions.

The more familiar we become with the mind the more we notice it, and in doing so we become increasingly mindful. It's a virtuous circle.

As we grow in mindfulness we start to learn the skill of accepting the junk and other destructive creations of the mind for what they truly are: just mental creations. Nothing special. Nothing to get concerned about.

We learn how to live with them, without being dragged by them to painful or aggressive places.

Over time we increase our ability to notice and just accept the existence of our various thoughts and emotions rather than be taken over by them.

We become increasingly at peace with the products of our mind, and feel calmer and more content as a result. Without a sense of want, or a sense of lacking something in our life we simply enjoy life.

Watch Where you Take your Mind

Increasingly the scientific evidence suggests that we are in a very deep sense guided by our genes, but our life experiences also influence how we feel about life, and how we respond to situations.

A very specific part of this is that, when we become adult and therefore more free of parental and school rules and influences, we tend to veer towards genetic-based preferences. These can be our interests and hobbies, careers, or simply habitual behaviours.

This might sound a little like we are fated to always be directed by inner drives, like a computer programme rather than a free being. This is true to some extent, and we should know and accept that this is the case.

But it's not the whole picture. Other evidence shows that, if we can sufficiently lean in other directions we can combat our genetic predispositions, if we want to, or cultivate new ways of doing, seeing, feeling.

This means that we can increasingly break free from our habits and inherited preferences if we want to.

Take for example handedness. I am left handed. Because this quality, which I inherited of course, is only found in a minority of people, many tools and objects designed for people are inherently right-handed. Most right-handed people won't even notice this, because the things they are using are so common. But left-handed people often notice.

Scissors are the classic example. They are designed to be used by the right hand, and simply don't work when using the left. More modern ones are better.

Most machines where you have to pay with coins e.g. drinks machines, are the same. The coin slot, which requires precision and dexterity, are almost always on the right hand side.

Ironically this biased way society works forces left-handers to practice more with their right hand than right-handers do with their left. So left-handers unconsciously become more ambidextrous than right-handers. And this is achieved purely through repeated practice.

So it is with all our habits. Practice, whilst rarely making perfect, certainly makes you better at skills. Additionally practicing the opposite of one skill can weaken the original skill you have developed. So practicing patience not only makes you more patient and considerate, it makes you less impatient and inconsiderate.

Think about what drains you, what harms you, and what you do that hurts others. List them. Then list their opposite traits. You now have a list of skills to practice through mindfulness! Just try to notice these qualities in moments when you are free to do so. Drop by drop the change will come.

Another Sort of Ambition

We live in what I think is a remarkably shallow and self-obsessed time, especially in the fields where I work, the world of business and professional careers.

Everyone seems to be urged to be more productive, hone their skills, commit to lifelong learning, aim for the top, fulfill their potential.

As they say in America "Anyone can become President" as if that means that everyone should try to achieve that aim.

Life, in my experience, has a habit of biting those who seek to live their life driven by such ambitions. Relatively recent political examples such as Tony Blair, David Cameron, and Michael Gove seem to suggest that if you want something a lot, and try to manipulate your way to that goal, life has a habit of snatching victory from you at exactly the worst time.

From a mindfulness point of view why might this be?

I'd suggest it's about focusing on the wrong target.

Mindfulness implies a simple and humble attention to the everyday, the mundane, the kinds of things that no one would ever be ambitious to notice or to achieve. After all who would achieve anything grand in life paying attention to what water feels like on your lips as you take a sip. Or how the heel of your foot feels as it touches the ground when you take a fresh step?

And yet...

When we do such practices, when we take our mind from shallow, self-satisfying dreams and visions, and turn our attention instead to the vivid if at first glance, unexciting present, we nurture certain qualities.

These are clarity of thought, the ability to discern between wisdom and foolishness in our mind, a stable calmness when considering matters, a deep sense of appreciation for all life and nature, and a sense of gratitude for being alive.

These in turn nurture a wider and deeper sense of compassion for all our fellow living beings.

As we develop these we start to gain greater clarity about a deeper sense of purpose, vision, ambition. Ambition, not for yourself, but for those around you.

And yes it is possible that fulfilling those ambitions for others may in fact reflect well on you in the eyes of others, and you may gain acclaim, promotion, high positions of power or income. But this would be an unintended consequences, not an aim in itself.

This is another kind of ambition altogether.

How Much of your Day do you Live?

Perhaps a better question than the one above might be "How alive are you during different parts of your day?"

How alive are you right now? In percentage terms. If being full of zest and love of life and fully engaged was 100% and feeling completely alienated from life and unable to see anything good was 0%. How would you score yourself right now?

Then think of a typical day in your life. There are periods when we're tired but that needn't mean a low score. If you're tired but know you're tired and have been able to find a quiet place to rest then you could still feel that deserves a high score. That's because you're *with* your tiredness, comfortable in it, knowing full well that this is the state you're in.

How are you when you watch a typical favourite TV programme? Are you fully engrossed, absorbed by the drama, or taken away to laughter by the comedy? If so that's being fully alive. That's a high score. But if you're half-tired, only partly watching out of habit while you flick through your messages on Facebook, then you're not really anywhere are you?

Just flitting from one dull level of attention to another. Not quite zombie, but not exactly inhaling the joy of being alive or even the bliss of resting when tired.

For those of you who work, try this out at different times of the working day.

Note the different scores you give yourself, and on reflection ask yourself, does this job enable me to live fully or does it in some way inhibit my ability to feel alive? We can do this for any moment of our day. It gives us insights into what types of activities are blocks to us living mindfully, that is fully and constructively.

That doesn't necessarily mean that the things you were doing when you scored yourself at the lowest levels are in themselves bad for you. It may be that you simply need to adjust how you perceive or engage with those activities, see them in a more positive light, fulfill the potential in them.

But it may be that certain things - hobbies, things you do with friends, some kinds of entertainment, some or even all of your work - are inherently drainers of your life. If you have any such life-killing activities it is important to notice them and do something about them.

Life has more than enough challenges without engaging in things that drain the energy from us.

But don't rush into changes. Take your time to see what can be improved or fixed, and what just has to go. Then think very carefully about what you might do as an alternative use of your time, especially if it's a job that's the problem, or a relationship.

The two important things to watch out for here are; not dropping what can be good in your life, and not staying trapped in by irredeemable obstacles.

The Impossible but Important Right Now

In a literal sense "right now" doesn't exist. As soon as you think the word "right" that moment has gone, but the moment relating to the second word "now" hasn't yet arrived. And once we've said the whole phrase "right now" it's in the past. Time waits for no one, as the old saying goes.

So when mindfulness is defined as "paying attention in the present moment" what does that mean in real life, and how can it be applied practically in our lives, especially if this thing – this idea – we call a moment is gone even as you think about it?

Part of the problem is the mind's constant urge to create thoughts, ideas, views, reactions. So for example we might see a robin perched on a park bench and the sight pleases us automatically (because we've evolved to like the sight of robins, or because our culture has conditioned us to think they are pretty).

Then our mind creates a thought "aw that's lovely". Now we're distracted. We have lost of the raw non-judging pleasure of seeing the robin and replaced it with our mental response to seeing it.

Then we hear it sing its tune. Again, for whatever reason, it gives us great pure pleasure. Then the thoughts emerge and take us away from the unadorned experience by the arising of words in our mind "what a beautiful tune".

Mindfulness is noticing this constant raw experience followed by a judgement or commentary. On noticing the thoughts arising we can with practice quickly see that we're being distracted from the very thing we're commenting on; in a way we're interrupting it and therefore the pleasure we were getting.

Assessing this we let our thoughts drop away and return to the pure sight or sound of the robin.

That's a very idyllic scene. I'd recommend you to try to have such experiences as often as you can. But it's when the destructive stuff emerges from your mind that this noticing comes to the rescue;

The moment when you get angry with your partner, colleague, children, parents.

The moment when you are about to dismiss someone's point of view without considering it;
The moment when you feel everything is terrible in your life and it's all someone else's fault;

The moment when you are cynical or self-centred or ignorant or faking it or just confused…

In these flashing moments we have an opportunity to witness the ugliness and unhelpfulness of what our brain has concocted, assess how harmful or useless it actually is, and let it go without letting it drag us its way.

So moments may seem impossible but they are always an opportunity, a field of potential.

Understand What you Can't Understand

Having caught up with the news headlines I was flicking channels this afternoon and came upon a Holywood film Nicolas and Alexandra about the life and deaths of the last Russian Czar and his family.

By the time I had found the film on the TV it was almost finished. The family had been arrested and sent to a kind of barracks. At one point one of the Czar's children, a boy, rushed to defend his elder sisters who were being harassed in a minor way by the revolutionary guards. A guard knocked him to the ground. Eventually everything settled down, no one was too hurt.I thought it was too cozy, unrealistic.

It made me think of a comment made by the mother of the American-Polish poet John Guzlowski. John was born in a Displacement Camp for Polish people who had been made slaves in Nazi Germany. His parents were slave labourers.

John once asked his mother, after they had watched Schindler's List together, what she thought of the film. She replied "They can't make movies about what really happened.".

My father, who spent eighteen months in a Soviet political labour camp said much the same thing to me. I said to him that if people really understood what had happened to the millions imprisoned and often killed in the Gulag camp system, they would see the world in a totally different way.

Dad replied "No one except those who were there can understand what it was like."

We can't know what we can't know. Mindfulness allows us to see when we wrongly think we do understand. When we assume other people's motives, feelings, perspectives.

Even more importantly, we can't even know the original cause or causes of our own mindsets, habits, perspectives; because every effect had a previous cause; and a previous one and so on until we're way back into assumptions about our genes, our ancestors, our human evolution.

We are mostly ignorant, in the neutral sense of that word. Yet we presume to know so much.

Mindfulness accepts our ignorance, rejects much of what rises in our mind as skewed and out of proportion to the reality of what has happened.

Few people have experienced what befell the Czar's or my father's family, or John's parents. Most of us have gripes with life which are very minor; yet we waste so much precious time on these.

We can't understand the scale of suffering some have to endure. But we can understand that most of what we spend precious time complaining about should just be allowed to slip into nothingness. Then we can get to what actually matters - noticing and enjoying the beauties of everyday moments.

When Interruptions Take Priority

I'm going to stop writing this in a minute.

Why?

Because one of our lovely cats has jumped up onto the desk and has his face in front of the keyboard.

Mindfulness does not suggest we routinely ignore or let go of distractions, negative emotions, interruptions. It means we notice what's actually going on.

In most cases a distraction will be considered not the best use of our time, so to gently notice it and let it fade away of its own accord, is a good decision. Using the breath as a point of focus is exceptionally helpful and practical to bring us back to the present reality, and act as a midpoint between the distraction and whatever we were hoping to focus on.

So the process would be:

mindless mind is distracted
mindful mind notices this
mindful mind gently focuses on breath
this allows distraction to fade away
mindful mind returns mind to original focus

In the real life case for me earlier today something else happened, as follows:

Cat jumped onto my desk
my mindless mind was distracted (ie. annoyed)
my mindful mind noticed this negative feel
my mindful mind saw what the reality was
the reality was my cat wanted affection
my mindful mind made a decision
decision: cat matters more than newsletter now
mindful mind changed focus to cat.

I'm not always as good as this example suggests. Often I've been annoyed by one of our cats and not recognised that what I was doing could in fact wait, and that both my cat and I would get a lot more out of the situation if I just patted him or her for a few minutes.

In that situation the moments were lost in annoyance, and an opportunity for a loving interaction slipped through my fingers. We also now know that interaction with pets nurtures good mental health, so that was lost too, ironically replaced by annoyance at a much loved creature.

We cannot control much of what affects us from the outside (like a cat jumping on our desk). Mindfulness helps us make wiser decisions in response to these situations. Reality - moment by moment - really is a field of potential. Use it well!

Your Very own Tea Ceremony

I was fortunate last year to go to Japan on holiday with my wife and daughter. It was a once in a lifetime trip and we made the most of it, visiting all the great sites, and trying some of the Japanese ways of living.

One of these is of course the Japanese Tea Ceremony. It's a very ornate yet slow, simple and elegant way of receiving and drinking tea, and expressing gratitude to the person who prepared the tea.

It wouldn't transfer over to our culture as there is so much that is uniquely Japanese about the experience.

However there are some things in the ceremony that we can use to enhance and develop our mindfulness practice whenever we have a drink of tea, coffee, water, even alcoholic drinks, though alcohol and mindfulness don't complement one another very much.

The first element is preparing the drink. In Japan it is elaborate. Here it's straightforward but there are several opportunities to be mindful.

Be aware of the fact that you - or your organisation if you do this at work - have a kettle; that the kettle was invented by a fellow human being, reflecting one of the great qualities of our species, creativity and original thinking. Understand that you have this quality too, even if you think you don't. It is nestled inside you. Don't question whether you have it. Just be aware of the thought that you do.

Next be aware that you are filling the kettle from a tap. Bring to your awareness the astonishing work done to enable each of us to have clear, pure water from a tap in the comfort of our own house or office. The amount of work and investment to have this in every home, every building, via reservoirs and purification plants is staggering.

This substance, water, keeps us alive more than anything we consciously take. In some lands people die from water-borne diseases every day.

Allow a sense of appreciation, gratitude or compassion - or all three - to just arise as you consider this. Don't worry if they don't appear. The practice is enough to start nurturing these qualities inside you.

Do the same when you pick up the coffee or tea bag. Consider all who were involved in planting, cultivating, picking, transporting, packing, unpacking and selling it so that you can enjoy this moment? Allow a sense of connection to these complete strangers to arise in you, and form the words "thank you" in your mind.

Finally enjoy a moment's silence, maybe even eyes closed, while you feel the warm cup in your hand, the first sip on your lips, then as it fills your mouth. This is your mindful tea ceremony. Appreciate it.

There is No Blank Slate

Sometimes, typically at New Year, we say we're going to turn over a new leaf. Give up drinking. Stop smoking. Stop being negative. Lose weight.

We've probably all done this and mostly, though not always failed.

We deluded ourselves that we can wipe the slate clean and start afresh.

Problem is, the slate is not clean. In fact the slate is so full it is impossible to see all that's in there.

The slate is, of course our own mind, and it is not blank, and never was.

At the moment we were conceived we started a process of life to death, a process which is a remarkable combination of conditioning and the potential to amend or override that conditioning.

The conditioning was not only created by the passing of our parents' genes to us, but by every single moment in our life, and it is still happening as you read this (and for me as I write this).

The brain absorbs the outside world through our five sense. These include not only sights and sounds etc, but ideas through reading or listening. These new inputs subtly, and occasionally radically, change our ways of thinking, doing, responding, reacting.
So the slate, never blank, keeps on being remoulded and reprogrammed.

In this respect therefore, practising mindfulness is a form of liberating ourselves from at least some of our programming; or perhaps at least gives us an opportunity to switch on purpose from one form of conditioning to another, healthier one.

We are, for example conditioned to be angry under certain circumstances. Yet we are also programmed to calmly accept difficult situations. We have the potential for both. Which one we respond with depends on our unique life circumstances; but mindfulness develops the ability to notice the conditioned response, let it go, and replace it with a more constructive one.

This is literally life-changing, moment by moment, and our ability to live in this mindful, skilful, discerning way grows stronger with practice and reflection on our real life, real time experiences.

So we don't have the privilege of wiping the slate clean and start with a blank one. We do however have the ability to, if you like, ignore one part of the filled slate that is prodding you to use it, and instead gently tilt your attention to a finer, more nurturing part of the slate. In doing so we change the complexion of our mind internally, and the nature of the ripple effect that is always caused by our reactions to situation.

Lonely at the Top - or the Perils of Making it Big

I read an unsurprising but saddening article in Forbes Magazine, the upmarket American business journal. It was from last year but I only just saw it on LinkedIn last week.

A survey of leaders of business organisations in America showed that they had double the rate of depression as the general population, which currently runs at 20%. So almost half have or have had depression. The survey also stated that they were even more prone to the most serious forms of depression. This is obviously awful for the individuals concerned and their families. It also begs some major questions.

Various reasons were suggested for the grim figures:
The macho culture of people who strive to stay ahead of the Joneses, measuring their self-worth against how others are faring.

The pressure of the job itself. A sense of isolation and loneliness at the top.

Finally, a much deeper cause was examined. A sense of emptiness, an absence of higher or more profound purpose. This is commonly found in people who have striven for years to achieve something; often they find not satisfaction but a huge sense of anti-climax on achieving their dreams.

As an old song goes "Is that all there is…?"

A related study from Britain says that 10% of the population are depressed in any given year. It is the leading cause of disability in men and women alike. Educationalists and teachers are reporting "an epidemic" of mental health issues in schoolchildren.

A third study found that 49% of start-up entrepreneurs had mental health issues, double the average for the population as a whole.

Contrasting these facts with the results of trials at Oxford University's Centre for Mindfulness are striking. They show that in patients with three or more previous episodes of depression – the group most at risk to have another episode - mindfulness reduces recurrence rates by 44% over a year.

Mindfulness has also been found to be highly effective in preventing depression and nurturing a sense of purpose, so that it can help business leaders, entrepreneurs and the general public from declining into depressive states of mind.

It is remarkably ironic that mindfulness - paying attention deliberately to everything, no matter how ordinary or tiny, has the effect of making people happier, calmer and kinder as well as more effective, whilst seeking "success" often harms our sense of wellbeing. Look carefully at your dreams, aims and goals. Review them so they work for your wellbeing, not just for your status.

Clear Understanding, Clear Practice

One of the biggest problems in developing a strong practice of mindfulness is the tendency to learn more and more *about* mindfulness instead of *practising* it.

This of course is common to many good habits in life. We become experts in good nutrition while still devouring chocolate bars and cakes. We read one self-help book after another but never implement the suggestions in any of them.

If we practise mindfulness without any understanding of the mind or the way our human mentality has evolved and been shaped by our genes and circumstances, we will still gain benefits.

However it's the combination, the ongoing ever-deepening interplay of understanding and practice that brings to full fruition the joys of living and the compassion for life and all that possesses it.

We have a great phrase in English, "in a nutshell". More appropriate for this subject though would be "in a skull". In the skull of a living human being is a remarkable thing called the brain.

Although some of the greatest people in history have given us the gift of wonderful insights about the mind, it is only very recently that we have begun to really understand some of how the brain works from moment to moment, and how in turn that affects who we are and how we behave.

So in a nutshell, in a skull, we now know from scientific findings that we have several unconscious biases, for and against people, things, groups. We have a negativity bias. Negative experiences *weigh* much more than good experiences eg. consider what you'd dwell on if you were given an appraisal and were told nineteen positive things and one thing you were rated poorly at performing. We know that the mind creates habits, good and bad, and these include emotion-habits like anger, self-doubt, depression, worry, bitterness, resentment and scores more which upset us and negatively affect our physical health.

Knowing these things helps when we *practise* mindfulness. The insights about ourselves gleaned from pure unadorned attention in moments can transform theoretical knowledge about the mind into real experience, connecting scientific knowledge to actual lived experience.

These real insights in turn can be used to more deeply understand the science.

It helps us put the facts into our own words, our own language. In this way we embed our understanding, giving us a series of anchors which help keeps us stable when the inevitable ups and downs of life come our way.

So to best use mindfulness to develop our finest qualities of mind, and diminish our destructive mental states, try to balance and interplay factual understanding and frequent momentary practice in your daily life.

Getting to Really Know your Emotions

The history of popular music is full of songs, some serious, some light-hearted, questioning what emotions really are, especially Love.

What is love?
I wanna know what love is
What is this thing called love?

We are so quickly and easily taken over by our emotions that we rarely stop to ask these questions. Some song titles and lyrics even hint at attempts to answer the questions:

Love is the drug
Anger is an energy

But while songs can be remarkably powerful and affecting they rarely help us go deeply enough inside ourselves to find actual answers to these questions, let alone solutions as to what to do about those emotions that cause challenges, sometimes crises in our lives.

Mindfulness starts with deliberately developing an intimate familiarity with our own mind (and our body and external things too).

Mindfulness is at this stage just getting to know the mind and all it produces, including emotions and views (often our views are deeply tinged with emotions - dislike, distaste, hatred, love, excitement, etc).

After 18 years of practicing mindfulness I still focus primarily on just noticing the products of my mind, how they arise, under what circumstances, how they sometimes sweep me away somewhere, how I sometimes let them fade away without being caught up, and how they always go away (even if they come back ten seconds later).

So, having looked at so much of what my mind produces, what can I say about our emotions?

Firstly they arise without any conscious effort or desire on your part.

Secondly, they arise so fast you can't stop them appearing.

Thirdly, they do go away even if you don't want them to.

From these observations, and scientific evidence, we can say that our emotions are mental creations which form into habits of mind, sometimes requiring an outside spark (eg. someone insults you), but often just spontaneously arising without any seeming cause.

From this we can conclude that we are not in control of what our mind creates - whether emotions, ideas, views - but we can learn not to accept what they bring to us. Just because we have an emotion doesn't mean we have to let it take over us. Mindfulness is the practice of gaining ever-greater mastery over all qualities of our mind.

When Thinking Becomes Ruminating

Thoughts have been of such immense benefit to us as a species. Ideas and the practical implementation of them have helped us create warm, safe homes, clean hot and cold water, plentiful supply of food, quality education, and medicines and medical procedures that save our lives.

However human thought has also been the direct cause of the Holocaust, the dropping of atomic bombs on Hiroshima and Nagasaki, and the recent tragedy of men, women and children drowning off the shores of Europe's favourite holiday spots in the Aegean and Mediterranean Seas.

At a more everyday level our thoughts sometimes start with something that niggles us or that we're unclear about. Within minutes these have blossomed into a multitude of linked ideas; one thought after another springing from the previous one in a downward spiraling chain of rumination, worry, frustration, into a mild despair or uncertainty.

From this we build a kind of surly or brooding mood that envelopes our body, facial expression, tone of voice.

Our friends, family and colleagues innately sense it and are wary of saying anything to us in case it brings forth a negative reply.

Many of us will have experienced this at difficult meetings at work.

This mood of course makes constructive and productive discussion virtually impossible, so the meeting peters out either with an unpopular decision being made, or more likely, nothing being concluded with no end result except a feeling that our precious time has been wasted.

It's the same at home when a similar mood has developed. This one priceless thing we have – time, made up of moments only – drains through our fingertips while our mood simmers.

Yet it is possible to dissipate this in seconds.

Just think to yourself what we do in our class, using our own breath as a focus, "Breathing in my mind feels clear. Breathing out it is calm and still".

Repeating these phrases a few times, or varying the key words, can completely shift our state of mind.

From this we can see the absurdity and problem everyone in the room is facing. They're all still caught up in the tense, unhappy mood that you were in until you broke free of it.

The next step depends on the situation and the culture of those around. In an ideal situation everyone has been trained in mindfulness so there's a common language and the potential for a common insight into the problem.

For others, suggesting a five minute break is often a way to lighten the situation. Suggesting we end the discussion and revisit it at a later date can also help. But none of this is possible unless you break your own ruminations and mood.

Mindfulness and Mindfulness Training: the Difference

Sometimes people confuse mindfulness and mindfulness training, and it's helpful to get the distinction right.

Mindfulness is one of the many qualities or states of mind our brain can produce. Other examples are anger, happiness, love, hatred, irritation, forgiveness. It's just not as well known as these others.

So there's nothing special about mindfulness but there is a lot that's special about what it can do for us in our daily lives.

Mindfulness is the skill or trained ability to notice what's actually going on, in a much wider and deeper sense than our usual autopilot sense of awareness.

With this particular skill of mindfulness we can avoid so many of our common poor decisions in life, which are the result of knee-jerk reactions to minor things, which we get way out of proportion.

On the positive side mindfulness allows us to see the potential for beauty or positive outlooks in everyday situations.

Thus we can avoid self-created situations and nurture moments of joy, happiness and kindness. It doesn't take a genius to work out how different that makes the quality of your day, and over time your whole life.

So mindfulness is the skill of noticing moment by moment in a much warmer, more open way.

Mindfulness training is what is says on the tin. It trains you to be increasingly more mindful. It does this by stepping out of the busyness of everyday life and guiding us to practice noticing what actually goes on moment to moment; usually focusing on our breath because that's always present, easy to notice, and easy to return to whenever we get distracted, bored or uncomfortable.

We also focus on the mind itself and what state it's in, on how parts of our body feel, on how words and mental images can positively affect how we feel. All of this is good practice for noticing more mindfully in normal life.

Over time our ability to be mindful increases, and this improvement can continue for life so long as we keep practicing and training.

The training is commonly referred to as "mindfulness meditation". To my mind meditation is a troublesome word. Many associate it with spiritual insights such as being one with the universe or God. The Buddha, who devised the techniques we call mindfulness, said his sole task was to teach about "suffering and how to end suffering." I'd be delighted to settle for that.

Understanding Yourself

There are two ways to learn something: academically and experientially.

By academic I mean through learning facts, knowledge, information. An example is to read the Lonely Planet Guide to Paris. If you do that diligently and repeatedly you can learn a huge amount about the city, its history, people, streets, restaurants, hotels, sites, and so on.

But if you haven't actually gone to Paris then you've missed something. In fact you've missed the bigger part, maybe the whole point of knowing Paris. Walking along the Seine, seeing the Eiffel Tower from various angles, sitting in a small café outside watching the local people go by. This too is knowing Paris, but in an entirely different way than through reading a book about it.

Mindfulness suggests that we learn about what's actually going on in the present moment, not academically through books or articles such as this, but through raw and immediate but calm and objective experience.

It is through repeated, long-term – indeed lifelong – calm, open observation that we learn through actual experiences what we are really like, what others are like, what society is like, and what nature and other aspects of the planet are like.

We are genetically and culturally programmed to seek to jump to conclusions as soon as possible. We see this in meetings or at home in discussions. We hear someone's opinions for the first sentence or two, then ignoring what they're about to say next, we reach a conclusion and blurt out our opinion.

Mindfulness asks us to do the opposite; to let go of the array of views and opinions and conclusions we reach, and instead just continue to observe as long as possible before contributing. It's not easy to do.

But the rewards are remarkable. We start to really get to know our mental traits, how they keep popping up, which ones don't feel pleasant, which ones cause unwanted outcomes; and which ones do feel pleasant, which ones do lead to positive or better than expected outcomes.

If we simply continue to practice being mindful, we will eventually become an absolute expert on our own mental production system – the brilliant and the junk and the terrible things our mind produces.

And we see what other people's minds produce.
And what life is actually like, using our five senses.
And how diverse human beings are, and nature is.

Unless we can truly know ourselves, accept it all, and work on engaging with only the finest qualities of our minds, we are prone to be dragged this way and that by our own thoughts and emotions.

When we really understand ourselves we can start to use our best qualities more and more of the time. Our life blossoms as we do so.

Dealing with Negative or Difficult People

We all consider some people in our lives as negative or difficult. They may be work colleagues, family members, friends, even our spouse or partner.

Mindfulness asks us to try to just notice; to try to gain a great deal of familiarity with our thoughts, emotional automatic reactions, and feelings (as well as external things we see, hear, touch, taste or smell).

When we get very familiar with our views of others many people find the same insights. Here are a few:

People we label negative or difficult are not always like that. They have moments of kindness, calmness, generosity. Sometime they are just silent, which at least gives you a reprieve from their negativity. Adolf Hitler, the number one candidate for worst human being of all time, was reportedly kind to animals and loved being with children.

From this we learn that - as with everything in mindfulness - it is not a negative or difficult *person* we are enduring, but rather a moment.

If we focus on moments rather than people as what is most important in our lives, then we can learn to readily deal with negativity or difficulty as it arises.

We simply note what the person said or did in that moment, mindfully assess how important or troublesome it *actually* is, as opposed to what our knee-jerk response tells us, and then, letting go of the instant reaction, determine with a clear mind what to do about the situation.

Most incidents are not nearly as big or terrible as our auto-reactions imply.

But some are: if the matter is truly serious, such as deep-rooted abuse of any sort, then you need to take direct action as soon as you can. Mindfulness is not about tolerating the unacceptable. In fact it helps bring clarity and decisiveness.

The other truly challenging, but more complex situation is when the negativity or difficulty is low-level but ongoing; insiduous, sneaky, affecting you drop by drop.

In this case you have to use your mindfulness to try to assess whether the other person is *deliberately* seeking to wear you out, undermine you, and hurt you. If so, it is a truly serious matter which needs addressed.

If on the other hand it is just an unconscious habit of the person then you need to very carefully, mindfully and compassionately assess whether it is so intolerant that you need to take real action to stop it or to leave so that you no longer need to face it; or whether it is in fact, with mindfulness practice, just a minor irritation in an otherwise enjoyable mutually-giving relationship.

So, get clear, assess accurately, then decide.

From Judging and Criticising to Reshaping

We moan when things don't go the way we want them to. Whether it's the weather, a traffic jam, a flight delay, or bad news, our minds are extraordinarily gifted at allowing words of complaint and feelings of annoyance to arise.

We judge people constantly. What do we feel about their clothes, shoes, hairstyle? Do they look their age? Older? Younger? What does their accent say about them? Are they people we like to be with, or folk we'd rather were on the other side of the planet?

Mindfulness tells us to simply notice these things as they pop up in our minds and are churned out one after the other. Doing this practice enables us to do two things; firstly, it helps us to not be swept away by the thought and feelings that make up the moan or the judgement. Secondly over time it makes us grow so familiar with the things our mind creates that we start to see them for what they really are: just a regular, repeating, automatically-created predictable response to everyday things in life.

We slowly really start to understand through sheer noticing that our mind just creates a bunch of stuff, some of which is useful, but much of which is useless at best and a nuisance or harmful at worst. From this we can learn to no longer accept our mind's responses to things unless, on reflection, we think what it has produced is really of benefit.

This isn't easy but we do get better at it over time.

The question then arises. If we don't think our moaning or our judging are useful in response to things that occur in everyday life, what are we to do about the things that we disliked happening or seeing in the first place?

This is where the brilliant recent concept of neuroplasticity can inspire us. Neuroplasticity means brain-shapability, for want of a better description. It means that through mindfulness and other activities we can change our brain and therefore our personality and characteristics. Plasticity means the ability to be moulded and remoulded into different shapes.

It's not only our minds that are "plastic" or changeable. Look at society; how much has changed in your lifetime? Don't allow your mind to tell you a list of "good" or "bad" examples. Just note that society too changes over time.

So, many things are plastic or changeable. You can play your part. Instead of judging, criticising or complaining about things, practise being creative. Start to waken up your mind's imagination and ask it "What would be better than these things I'm moaning about or judging? How could we change things for the better?" Whether it's a suggestion at work to avoid everyone getting stressed, or a vision to change society, it requires us to make the shift from our default judging mind to a reshaping, creative one. Go for it; it makes life much more interesting!

When Tired, Rest

Whether you are at work or home there is a remorseless expectation that when you are tired you should just soldier on, work through it.

That's such a wasteful, pointless, self-defeating mentality, sometimes imposed by the culture of your family or workplace, but even more commonly self-imposed.

It's also tied into how the mind and doing things work together. The mind gets into a rhythm of doing work or some other activity, and even when the mind or body start to tire, the mind itself wants to continue the rhythm it is now accustomed to.

And what the mind wants we unthinkingly do.

But our quality of attention suffers, our pace of work reduces, our state of mind gets more irritable and intolerant.

So what we produce – whether that's some form of work, or just a chat we're having - once we're tired it is of significantly poorer quality than when our mind is sharp, clear and calm.

I know it is very difficult in some workplaces to just close your eyes at your desk or go out for a walk. But even a change of attention from the harsh light of your laptop screen to the flow of air lightly passing through your nostrils and into your lungs can make a near-instant improvement in how you feel.

Doing it three of four times for a minute or two can make a huge difference to how you're feeling.

Tiredness isn't only associated with poor performance or low productivity. It's also correlated with being more snappy, grumpy, and irritable. We simply don't have the energy to bear with patience anything that isn't exactly how we want it to be.

This makes us unpleasant company for those around us; and in a work context it makes it less likely that communication will be good as people will avoid you if you are in that sort of mood.

So all told, tiredness is a terrible state, and only you can take responsibility for ensuring you don't inflict it on yourself or make those around you suffer from how it makes you behave.

The core of tiredness is of course poor sleep: poor quality and poor quantity. We tend to try to squeeze as much out of our last waking hours as possible, but this is a false economy.

It is far far more productive for our daily lives to turn that thinking around completely. Sleep should be a top priority. If in doubt go to bed early, not late. Wake up refreshed. Wake up relishing the prospect of a new day, a new set of opportunities, challenges, fun.

Joy

It's a tiny word isn't it? A wee word that describes one of the most special feelings we can experience as a human being. A feeling many people very rarely experience, and, sadly, a feeling many people don't even think about ever experiencing.

You can't fake it. You can, and many of us have, faked happiness, feeling pleased, for ourselves or for others. It's something many of us do almost as a social custom: "I'm so pleased for you." "I'm fine thanks" "Yes, all's good thanks." People often hide behind such phrases when it fact they don't feel particularly happy. I don't think there's anything wrong with this, in fact it can be helpful or at least allow us not to get caught up in a long conversation when we don't have the time.

But it is pretty hard to imagine faking joy. Joy is in a different league altogether. Joy isn't the same as being excited. It's more like a sense of bliss, being elated.

Right now, if feeling joy scored you 100 and feeling miserable gave you a score of zero, what score would you give yourself right now in terms of how you feel. Try not to exaggerate, in either direction. A score of fifty is if you're feeling OK but neither happy nor unhappy.

It's good sometimes just to check in and sense your mood in this way. Some of us - whether through our genes or our life experiences - have a more sombre or downbeat default state of mind than others, and this is fine.

However I have noticed personally that my own slightly over-serious normal mood can tire me a bit, and make me perceive things critically rather than constructively.

This is where the real life, moment by moment practice of mindfulness helps me so much. I notice my mood, maybe score it a 35 out of 100. I can laugh at this now; I see it so often.

And then I smile.

Or notice my breath.

The life-giving freshness of the in-breath, and the warm gentle flow of the outbreath.

And this wakes me up to the realisation that I am fully alive.

And sometimes; sometimes joy just appears. Accompanied by an enormous sense of gratitude for being alive, being able to experience existing.

I didn't try to attain joy. I didn't even think about it. It wasn't on my radar at all. It just comes, like a gift from life itself, like a visitation from something very beautiful. But it comes from inside me, not outside.

And I gain an insight: Joy is a result. A result of noticing more and more clearly, allowing the junk product of our mind to fall away. It is our ongoing practices of being mindful that creates joy.

Happiness is a Choice, Not a Result of Doing Things

We tend to link our happiness with doing certain things or achieving certain goals.

Major life examples include meeting the right person, getting a nice home, getting our income to a particular level.

What is certainly true is that the absence of certain things make it virtually impossible to attain happiness: hunger and thirst, extreme pain, particularly harsh noises, realistic fear of imminent danger or violence. It is very difficult to bring happiness to such circumstances.

On a more everyday level we think that if we can finish a specific task then we'll be able to relax and be happy. Those of us who work think like this all the time. We feel the pressure to get something done and only then can we relax and be happy again. So we delay happiness until then.

Yet the science that underpins mindfulness suggests an entirely different possibility, and experience of practice backs this up.

Thich Nhat Hanh put it best when he said (I paraphrase) that happiness is too important for us to wait until the conditions are right. Instead we should *choose* to be happy right now.

So part of your moment by moment mindfulness practice is to try to separate out what you do or want to do from how you feel at any moment. This isn't easy as our minds want to link the two all the time. It says "Your happiness depends on getting this done". It's simply not true.

Instead, use being mindful from moment to moment to check out your state of mind, regardless of what you're doing or hoping for. If your mind is not happy or healthy, let that state (or thought or feeling) fade away, and replace it with awareness of the breath or your feet on the ground, or the sounds around you.

That brings you from a negative to a neutral mind, maybe even better than neutral because these simple sensations - the breath, the feel of feet on the ground, many sounds - are pleasant. Even better, with practice and familiarity they can feel more and more pleasant as soon as you notice them.

Then simply choose happiness. Do a little inner smile. Notice that you are alive. Choose to appreciate this. Choose to feel grateful for life and all you have that is good and safe and healthy. This works, and gets easier to reach with practice.

What you do, do.

Review your plans occasionally, to ensure they will nurture you and those around you, or that they'll be fun. But don't link these to your happiness.

Your happiness is a separate matter, a matter of mental choice, a result of mindfully noticing our state of mind and deciding to adjust it if it's not helpful.

Who is it that has Emotions and Moods?

A classic statement in mindfulness and CBT amongst other ways of seeing things is the view "You are not your thoughts". This is often a revelation to people for the simple reason that no one had previously pointed this out to them. Moreover it can be an extremely helpful way of understanding our relationship to our own emotions and feelings, as well as ideas and views. In short it gives us permission not to accept our feelings and thoughts as being necessarily correct or helpful at any given time.

But the statement does give rise to some fundamental questions; questions which can be of even greater help than the first revelation itself.

If you are not your thoughts then two immediate questions spring to mind:

What then *are* your thoughts?
and Who are *you* if you are not your thoughts?

This might seem to be taking us down paths that lead to pointless conjectures and academic discussions but bear with me. I think it can take us in a completely practical and helpful path.

Let's start with the first question: what are your thoughts?

In a nutshell they are the automatic arisings - feelings, ideas, views, memories, whatever - of your mind.

They are caused by an almighty mix of your genes and every single experience you have ever had. These, in conjunction with the human body and mind, conspire to create this endless flow of mental creations we call thoughts, moods, opinions, views, feelings, emotions.

So let's look at the second question now: who are you if you are not your thoughts?

At one level we can honestly say, we *are* just our thoughts, moods, views, characteristics (if we exclude the body for a moment). But not just our *automatic, knee-jerk reaction* ones.

It's true that our mind produces these automatic, often harmful or unpleasant thoughts and feelings, and this is who we are as a result.

But the mind also allows us to notice our own mental creations, judge whether they are helpful or not, and disarm them subtly and skillfully if they seem unhelpful.

It is this latter part of the mind - the wiser, calmer, more considerate function of the mind that we all like to think is our *real* self. It's our best nature.

I think we can build and nurture this more refined mind through practices of mindfulness. and I am certain that we will build these qualities more quickly and strongly if we have confidence that we are building our true self, our full potential this way.

Update and Restart

Sometimes when we try to switch off our computer more than the usual options appear. One of these is Update and Restart. It's a very good analogy for doing one of the most effective mindfulness practices I know.

Most mornings I remember to look at my state of mind when I wake up. Often it's fine; not particularly cheery or happy but pretty alert and looking forward to the day. But sometimes it's a combination of uncertainty about why I'm doing what I'm doing that day, plus a low-level but still noticeable anxiety that I won't get certain things done.

This frame of mind is rarely an accurate prediction of what I do get done that day. It's just a fear-based mental habit that occurs because, well, that's what the mind sometimes chooses to do. Knowing precise causes of what arises in the mind is often impossible, and in any case is rarely useful. In fact often it becomes a long-running distraction from what does matter, living and noticing in the present moment.

Even if it is an accurate assessment of your day ahead, uncertainty and anxiety are not helpful emotions to have when you start your day.

So what I do is, firstly notice my state of mind. Often this is the hardest thing to do, as I am sure you'll be very aware.

I then think to myself "what state of mind would I prefer to have right now?" and the answer is almost always the same.

A mind that is happy – not deliriously so, not cheesy, not partying – just content, and filled with a love of life, and an appreciation that I am actually alive to experience this life, this world.

And I want a mind that is at peace.

And a mind that feels kind and considerate towards other people and to other living things.

So then I do a short practice, maybe a minute or two or three. Breathing in I think "breathing in I feel happy being alive" or some variation on those words. I think of my home, my family, the trees and sky and pleasures of life. And the happiness starts to take the place of the uncertainty.

On the outbreath I think "I am at total peace".

I do these two practices for a few rounds of the breath then drop the "at peace" one and replace it with "Breathing out I wish kindness and consideration to everything that lives". You don't need to use the same words I choose; use words that actually reflect what you want to feel.

That's it. In this way, in a few minutes I have updated my mental programme, and restarted it in the right frame of mind for the day ahead.

Work ON your Life as well as IN your Life

One of the classic business guru books was called the E-Myth, by Michael E Gerber. In a nutshell he said that for a business to really succeed the owner-manager needed to spend their time working ON the business rather than just IN the business.

The general reasoning was that, for any of our endeavors to flourish, we need to take time out from our everyday busy activities to consider how best to nurture and grow it.

Setting aside the fact that all sorts of other issues require to be looked at in the world of business - from overall purpose, inequality, exploitation, harmful products, etc - this principle is important, and is in some ways similar to mindfulness.

For us to flourish in our lives through mindfulness we need to take time away from our busy routines in order to practice; to get sufficient time to practice deliberately noticing what is actually going on in the moment. We need to do this for two reasons:

to get better at noticing - through practice.

to gain insights about your life, your mind, your mental habits, and about others in life.

We then need to build our endeavor, which is to nurture our finest mental qualities so that we can live as full, healthy, enjoyable and kindly life possible, making the most of this unique adventure we can being alive.

What makes this practice different from the E-Myth is that mindfulness then says we have to go back into everyday life and live it more fully, more freely, and more enjoyably.

Mindfulness is not a practice of running away from normal life. It's not even some sort of occasional refuge from the strains of work and family and money, even though we can all benefit from that.

It's a way of building your wisdom, a way of helping you see your own life, the lives of those around you, and life itself in the big sense of that word, in a more vibrant, open-minded, and clear-sighted way.

It's about seeing beauty and wonder in your everyday life, in what we normally consider bland, dull things. William Blake put it incredibly powerfully:

"To see a world in a grain of sand
And a Heaven in a Wild Flower

Hold Infinity in the palm of your hand,
And Eternity in an hour."

And that's the great difference between Gerber's business building method and mindfulness. Gerber sees that a business has to grow, to be made bigger and more powerful in order for it to be deemed fulfilled. Mindfulness seeks to let us see that so much in life is astonishing exactly as it is. We just need to see things differently.

The Moral Philosophy of Mindfulness

Mindfulness fully understood and practised is not just something that exists on its own. In common with virtually every religion, at least in principle, it rests on the principle of "do no harm".

And of course most of us would instinctively agree with this. Few people would willingly hurt another living thing. But we all have our unique genes and life experiences, upbringing and local or national cultures, so our interpretation of this "golden rule" varies enormously depending on who we have become.

In pure scientific terms it is impossible to stay alive and not harm something.

We need to breathe, and in this process we take in microscopic living things in the air, killing some of them in the process.

We need to drink, and, as with the air, water carries with it microscopic organisms, which again, we harm or kill by drinking.

Most of us would never think of this when we consider not harming as a basic principle in our lives.

But the next step is where it gets tricky and challenging. We need to eat, and most things we eat were at one stage a living thing.

Fruit comes from a living thing but isn't itself living when it falls or is picked. Vegetables on the other hand, especially root vegetables, are living until we pick them.

But plants, so far as we know, don't feel pain, so if we define "harm" as causing pain, physical or mental, then plants don't come into it.

It's when we bring animals, birds and fish into the exploration that things become very sensitive. Our culture has made us think of meat, fish and poultry as just products on a shop, not parts of what were once living, and often intelligent and sensitive animals.

We can consider how we might hurt people without meaning to - in our tone of voice, in a look, simply because we are gloomy or tired on a certain day.

Finally, and very importantly, we should not harm ourselves. We self-harm in all sorts of seemingly innocent ways. Accepting without question particular views we grew up with, views of ourselves that hamper us, that say we can't succeed in certain areas; or deep-rooted habits that damage our health, our happiness, our relationships.

Mindfulness is rooted in this principle of "do no harm" but it doesn't prescribe answers to the questions about what is or isn't harmful. That's your life task. Mindfulness just helps you see better whether something is or isn't harmful, and helps you think more clearly when consider what to do about the insights you gain from being mindful.

Freeing Yourself Wherever you are

I have a lovely little book called Be Free Where You Are, by Thich Nhat Hanh. Hanh is one of the most revered Zen teachers alive, friend of Martin Luther King, and a man who personally saved hundreds of people in his long life. It's a tiny little book, only 80 pages long, and less than half the size of a standard paperback.

But it is awesome, and so insightful.

It's a transcript of a talk he did at a maximum security prison in America several years ago. He talked about freedom of the mind. In particular freedom **from** the mind.

In other words, freedom from the destructive, unhelpful and draining things the mind creates automatically in response to things going on in our lives, or even created seemingly from nothing.

We can understand just how radical a way of looking at our lives, and the idea of what freedom actually is, when we see it presented in this way; to prisoners, most of whom are locked up for life, some presumably on Death Row.

One can't imagine much that is further from our idea of freedom than how those prisoners live.

Yet Thich Nhat Hanh in the book says that we are all imprisoned. Imprisoned by our automatic thoughts, feelings, prejudices, hates, even our hopes, dreams, desires.

We are imprisoned by these because we are stuck with them and we don't control the mind that creates them, so we are at the whim of a remarkable thing that sways us this way and that; and we are blinkered and blocked by fixed ways of seeing ourselves and others.

So in literal terms my genes, my DNA prevents me from flying like a bird and in this way I am limited. But the same genes added to my life experiences make me irritable driving a car, which limits my enjoyment of driving. My birth and upbringing in Scotland makes me see things through a "Scottish" viewpoint, thus England's football results take on a significance that would not be the case if I was born in Poland where my father came from.

Mindfulness says we should aim to free ourselves from all limiting, narrowing, and blinkered perspectives, because these views reduce our experience of being fully alive.

Some of our mental habits - stress, anxiety, worry, hate, bitterness, anger - not only poison our minds and destroy precious moments, but slowly consume our body and cause us illness and often an early death.

Thich Nhat Hanh believes prisoners in jail for life can be free simply by reframing - or maybe better to call it deframing - their minds. So observe your mind, see where the chains are, the locked cell doors that limit and restrain you from living a fuller happier life; and let them disappear with practice.

Conditioning and Handling it

Some of you may have noticed that the Olympics Games were on and have just finished. The BBC covered it all as normal and a huge emphasis was on how well the British sports men and women did at these games. Every day someone in the British team did something "historic" while the competitors from the more than two hundred other countries involved barely got a mention. Only Ussain Bolt's remarkable achievements stole the headlines away from British successes.

To put this in perspective there were 306 gold medals up for grabs, and Britain won 27. How many of the competitions which Britain didn't win, or get a medal in, were shown on TV?

Everything conditions us. Absolutely everything. This is how the brain works. It takes in anything and everything then sorts it into some sort of order from which to make sense of the world, so that we may going about our day from a sort of created vision of what the world and life is.

Undoubtedly most other countries were doing what Britain did, focusing almost exclusively on their own athletes' feats.

This conditions all of us to think from a parochial, national point of view rather than seeing the whole picture.

Not all conditioning is bad. Our genes produce conditioned thinking and feeling, some of which are essential to our survival. The feelings of hunger and thirst are conditioned into our brain.

Hunger is an interesting condition because it changes with experience. If you regularly have three meals a day and snacks in between but happen to miss one snack today your brain will register "hunger" even though you are not in need of food. The routine of eating at particular times has conditioned your brain to experience hunger based on past eating habits. So you get a false warning sign in response.

Mindfulness is the skill of noticing, and much of what we can notice is our conditioning. If we don't notice it we can't assess whether the conditioning is nurturing, neutral or harmful to us or people around us.

So noticing is key.

Once we notice, especially if we see the same kinds of conditioning arising regularly, we are better able to let go of any negative ones.

It is difficult to completely eradicate types of conditioning but we can learn to disarm them as they arise, and to be cautious about our own views when subjects arise about which we know that we have an unhelpful conditioning.

Most of us have racial, gender, age, national and political conditioned views – amongst many others - which are inaccurate and unfair to others. This is normal but it doesn't mean we should let them flourish. Let them go and they will weaken.

Deal with Issues as if you are Drinking Tea

Everyone has heard of the Japanese tea ceremony. I've been lucky enough to be part of one. It seems very elaborate and full of ritual, with lots of slow bowing and passing on of cups from one person to another.

Everything is in order and has its place. From the minimalist floral decoration, to the position of the cup at the table, everything is where it should be, and everyone knows how things should be.

The drinking of the tea is just part of the ceremony. The preparation and the display, the atmosphere and the respect shown to all are as important.

Kindness, attention, and appreciation are the key human qualities everyone is asked to bring; and each of these should be both light and understated.

Imagine if your meetings at work were planned like this; or if your attitude at home with family were even a little bit more like this than normal.

Imagine if we were able to handle a full-blown crisis in this manner.

Let's face it. Most of us are a million miles from this. Everything is fine until the problem hits the fan. Someone panics; someone else starts blaming a colleague or a relation. Someone gets upset and feels picked on.

At work, egos are on parade, with some people trying to show how tough they are in a difficult situation. People at meetings vie to be heard, unlistening, just poised to butt in when the current speaker pauses for a breath.

Imagine a tea ceremony was like that. No one would notice the taste or aroma or temperature of the tea at all. The purpose of the ceremony would be destroyed in an instant. No one would gain anything from it.

This is what so much of our lives dealing with situations are like. Instead of a serene, effective tea ceremony, we have a riotous Mad Hatters Tea Party.

A mindful approach to this has two phases.

First, sort yourself. Train, practice regularly, at every moment you remember to do so. This is your preparation for future issues, for your tea ceremony.

Second, where you can, start to encourage, train or tell others that this is how we handle issues. We train our minds; we know what is acceptable and what is not; and we approach matters with kindness, attention and appreciation of one another.

In this way, most crises can feel like and be managed by all involved, as if a tea ceremony.

When Something Annoying Occurs

It happens.

No matter how smart we are, how intelligent, how thoroughly prepared – still, every so often, something happens that we didn't want or expect.

I had this earlier today. (I'm writing this on Friday evening).

The law firm of which I am Director of Culture and Communications was looking for a new Marketing Manager and we found the perfect candidate. She was due to start on Monday but phoned our HR Director this morning to say she has had a change of heart.

Two factors made her change her mind, neither to do with our firm. One was a personal, family matter; the other an offer from the organization she currently works for.

We had planned two days of induction, involving over a dozen people, to be followed by three weeks of a transition between the departing marketing manager and the new one.

When I was told the news my mind instantly responded with (and here's where the asterisks come in very handy):

Jesus Christ. F*****g hell. How the hell did that happen?

I don't mean to shock anyone with that response – those were quite simply the exact words that appeared in my mind, propelled by the forces we call anger and frustration.

I didn't actually say those words. But that wasn't due to my mindfulness, just our usual discipline of self-restraint that usually happens at work.

However after that I did become mindful.

I recognized that my anger, frustration, and certainly the swear words would hinder not help the situation.

So I just watched my mind and in a few seconds the anger and frustration subsided, to be replaced with a clear mind.

No solutions, just a clear mind. But with a clear mind I was then able to ask open questions, consider various options, and we found what appeared to be a good potential solution.

Two phone calls and one hour later everything was resolved.

There's a bit more work to be done but what seemed like a crisis and a major stumbling block was seen as what it actually was, a minor problem, fairly easily resolved – by being mindful.

Printed in Poland
by Amazon Fulfillment
Poland Sp. z o.o., Wrocław